MILEPOST

The Golden Years of
British Steam Trains
GWR

GREAT WESTERN RAILWAY

MILEPOST

INTRODUCTION

Unlike its three rival companies, the Great Western - which dated back to the 1830s - retained its identity and absorbed a range of smaller constituent railways, principally in South Wales with such companies as the Taff Vale and Rhymney.

Locomotive development was therefore a continuous process which evolved logically throughout the nineteenth century and continued to do so until nationalisation in 1948.

Whereas the climax of motive power development occurred during the 1930s/40s in the other companies, the Great Western's final phase began at the beginning of the century with Churchward's 4-6-0 Saints and Stars. These formed a bedrock for the remainder of the company's existence and ensured a high degree of standardisation. The Saints gravitated to the Halls; the Stars to the Castles; and the Castles to the Kings.

Apart from being generic, the Great Western's locomotives were extremely handsome ; nineteenth century designs were characterised by outside frames, whilst the twentieth century ones had a very modern business like appearance. Brass chimney bands and safety valves, glorious brass number plates and name plates, green locomotives and brown and cream coaching stock endeared the railway to the general public and enthusiasts alike. It's long tradition of superb engines attracted a cult following and it was the most passionately loved of the Big Four group.

At nationalisation, the Great Western handed over 3,857 locomotives covering 60 principal classes with much of this diversity representing the tail end of the legacy inherited from the smaller absorbed railways.

Previous spread
End of the line in every sense - 0-6-0PT No. 3725 takes water at Bromyard shortly before closure in September 1964. Until 1952, the line had continued on as far as Leominster. The engine did not long outlive the branch, being withdrawn in January of 1965.

Modified Hall Class 4-6-0 No. 7905 "Fowey Hall" stands at Penzance Station with the 6.40 p.m. mail train to Paddington.

War Department Austerity 2-8-0 No. 90363 heads a freight train through the Brunel designed station at Culham between Didcot and Oxford.

King Class No. 6026 "King John" in double chimney form, stands at Shrewsbury with the Cambrian Coast Express from Paddington. The train will be worked forward from this point by smaller engines.

Hawksworth 0-6-0PT No. 8487 stands at the buffer stops of Paddington's platform 1 having brought empty stock from Old Oak Common for a down express.

Busy scene at Birmingham Snow Hill as 4-6-0 No. 6854 "Roundhill Grange" enters on an up excursion. Sadly, this fine station was closed and demolished in 1972 and only in recent years has a small substitute appeared for local services.

Bound for Ruabon and the Midlands, 2-6-0 No. 6311 crosses the Mawddach Estuary on the approach to Barmouth Junction having followed the coast from Dovey Junction to Morfa Mawddach.

Opposite
1400 Class 0-4-2T No. 5811 bowls a two coach train along the scenic branch from Bala to Blaenau Festiniog.

Tyseley based 0-6-0PT No. 3625 emerges from the stygian gloom of the tunnel and runs light into Birmingham Snow Hill Station.

Another light engine movement in the form of 0-6-0PT No. 4671 caught standing at Severn Tunnel Junction Station.

The Castle Class 4-6-0's were overwhelmingly named after castles although some earls, a few notable people and famous aircraft of the R.A.F. were also commemorated as in this picture showing Reading based No. 5076 "Gladiator".

Previous spread
The Mayflower - 8.30 a.m. Plymouth to Paddington - made its first stop at Exeter St. David's where it is seen arriving behind a King Class 4-6-0.

Severn Tunnel based Churchward 2-8-0 No. 2826 drifts slowly beside bridge engineering works.

On a wet day at Shrewsbury No. 7823 "Hook Norton Manor" heads the down Cambrian Coast Express.

A double chimney King leaves Paddington in December 1962 with a down express for Wolverhampton.

William Dean's Barnum Class 2-4-0s were introduced on to the Great Western in 1889. They had sandwich frames and were extremely successful engines. Here we see No. 3223 preparing to turn at Gresty Lane, having worked into Crewe from Wellington. This example survived until 1936, the class becoming extinct the following year.

A Hawksworth County Class 4-6-0 makes a business like departure from Penzance with the up Cornishman.

Tyseley based 0-6-2T No. 5647 heads a West Midlands freight train. Two hundred of these freight hauling tanks were built between 1924 and 1928 primarily for service throughout the vast coalfields of South Wales.

Opposite page
A Churchward Class 43XX, 2-6-0 heads the Hastings to Birkenhead through train amid the outer suburbs of Birmingham.

One of the popular Saint Class 4-6-0's No. 2924 "St. Helena" enters Exeter St. David's with a north to west express, the formation including two ex-L.N.W.R. carriages. Built in 1907, No. 2924 lasted until 1950.

Duke Class 4-4-0 No. 3252 "Duke of Cornwall" stands in Shrewsbury Station in April 1935. Built in 1895 it was withdrawn in 1937 being replaced by a Dukedog 4-4-0.

Castle Class 4-6-0 No. 4095 "Harlech Castle" of Plymouth Laira Shed, stands in Bristol Temple Meads Station with an up empty stock train.

Churchward Class 43XX, 2-6-0 No. 7305 of Banbury Shed, stands at Leamington Spa General on a down stopping passenger train in August 1960. The camera wielding enthusiast seems totally absorbed in the proceedings.

A double chimneyed Castle Class 4-6-0 on arrival at Paddington with the tightly timed Bristolian express. During the summer of 1959 this train was scheduled to cover the 118 miles between Paddington and Bristol in 100 minutes.

Opposite page
Another double chimneyed Castle at Worcester Shrub Hill on the up Cathedrals Express to Paddington.

0-6-0ST No. 1331 was a former Whitland and Cardigan Railway engine taken over by the Great Western in 1886. Built by Fox Walker & Co. in 1877, it was re-built at Swindon in 1927 and after a spell working on the Weymouth Harbour Tramway, it was transferred to Oswestry where this picture was made. The veteran was finally withdrawn in 1950.

1076 Class double framed 0-6-0PT No. 1574 was built as an 0-6-0ST in 1879 and rebuilt to the form seen here in 1927. Caught shunting at Oxford, No. 1574 was one of the last survivors of this large class and remained in service until 1937. Note the typical G.W.R. shunter's truck.

0-6-0PT No. 9700 was the first of eleven pannier tanks to be fitted with condensing gear for working over Metropolitan Railway sub-surface lines to the G.W.R. depot at Smithfield. The engine is seen at Old Oak Common Shed.

Ex-M.&S.W.J.R. 2-4-0 No. 1334 at Didcot on 11th May 1936. No. 1334 was one of three engines built by Dubs & Co. in 1894 and fitted with a G.W.R. standard boiler in 1924. These engines were used on the branch from Newbury to Lambourne.

Another double framed 0-6-0PT No. 1565 at Didcot, also on 11th May 1936. This example is fitted with a spark arresting chimney for working in local military stores depots. It survived until 1938.

The Dukedogs were a hybrid of Duke type boilers on Bulldog frames. These lively 4-4-0 s were light enough to work on lines such as those in the Cambrian section over which many larger engines were forbidden. No. 3212 "Earl of Eldon" is seen new at Swindon in May 1937. This engine was only named for a few weeks as its nameplates were transferred to the Castle Class 4-6-0 No. 5055 in July 1937.

Class 14XX, 0-4-2T No. 1401 stands in the bay of the decrepit looking Banbury Station which was to be re-built in B.R. days. No. 1401 was in charge of a push and pull train to Chipping Norton and Kingham.

Another Class 14XX, 0-4-2T No. 1424 stands in Gloucester station with a Chalfont train. This service ceased at the end of 1964 and was the last push and pull working on former G.W.R. lines.

The happy days of the School Treat are beautifully captured here by Arthur Mace. Invariably the excursions would be by train and performing the honours on this occasion is an 0-6-0PT.

Previous spread
Birmingham Snow Hill was one of Britain's best loved stations. It's architecture, it's light and shade effects, it's bustling atmosphere and glorious diversity of trains endeared it to the nation. Much of the magic is caught here as a King Class 4-6-0 arrives on a Birkenhead to Paddington express.

Churchward's first 2-8-0 was built in 1903 and by 1919 there were 84 in service. Remarkably, between 1938 and 1942, a further 83 similar engines were built. No. 3842, seen on an unfitted freight train, was one of the later built engines.

Wolverhampton Oxley based 0-6-0PT No. 9630 marshalling a freight train. Note the G.W.R. Toad brake van behind the engine.

Oxford based Hall Class 4-6-0 No. 6956 "Mottram Hall" approaches the outskirts of Birmingham with a down inter regional express.

Modified Hall No. 6992 "Arborfield Hall" enters Worcester Shrub Hill with an up Hereford express.

Previous spread
Castle Class 4-6-0 No. 5046 "Earl Cawdor" enters Shrewsbury with a down train during the early 1960s.

On 27th April 1963 the semi-final of the F.A. cup was played at Aston Villa's ground. It brought 15 special trains from the Southampton area to Birmingham Snow Hill, all but one being hauled by Bulleid light Pacific's. Three of the football specials went via Worcester and were piloted by Class 8F 2-8-0's from Stourbridge. One of these, No. 48478, has assisted No. 34009 "Lyme Regis" on the 07.10 a.m. from Southampton. As the supporters leave Snow Hill Station the fireman stands in the Pacific's tender shovelling coal forward.

It's thumbs up from the train spotters eagerly awaiting the specials as No. 34088 "213 Squadron" heads the 08.49a.m. from Southampton Central into Birmingham Snow Hill.

Un-rebuilt Bulleid Pacific No. 34094 "Mortehoe" enters Birmingham Snow Hill with the 08.00 a.m. special from Southampton Central.

This delightful veteran was built by Sharp Stewart of Manchester in 1866. Numbered 1197, she was one of three 2-4-0Ts constructed for the Cambrian Railways and is seen in Oswestry Shed. She survived until 1948.

Three of the six 1934 built 1366 Class 0-6-0PTs in the stock shed at Swindon. Their main use was shunting those sidings in the works that required short wheel base engines and also on the Weymouth Harbour Tramway. In their final years they replaced the veteran Beattie 2-4-0Ts at Wadebridge for the line to Wenford Bridge.

At Towyn on the Cambrian Coast Line, the 2' 3" gauge Talyllyn Railway is within easy access of the G.W.R. station. Talyllyn Railway 0-4-0WT "Dolgoch" of 1866 vintage stands at the line's Abergnolwyn terminus.

Castle Class 4-6-0 No.5046 "Earl Cawdor" - a Wolverhampton Stafford Road engine - has arrived at Shrewsbury

Dukedog 4-4-0 No. 9017 and a highly polished Manor 4-6-0 stand in Shrewsbury Station having been rostered to work the Cambrian Coast Express.

Castle Class 4-6-0 No. 4078 "Pembroke Castle" in the up centre road at Bristol Temple Meads with two coaches to be added to the formation of an up Weston Super Mare express.

At the buffer stops at platform 1 Paddington where Hawksworth 0-6-0PT No. 9415 has brought in the empty coaches for the 11.30 a.m. Penzance departure. These were one of the last Great Western designs to be built; they were ordered at the end of 1947, immediately before nationalisation, and building continued into the early 1950's.

An Oswestry based Dean goods 0-6-0 No. 2424, heads a stopping passenger train. This engine escaped military service and was withdrawn in 1946.

The famous Bulldogs were introduced in 1898. They had a wonderful variety of names ranging from places in the British Empire, birds, notable rivers and famous celebrities. Most of the nameplates were of the traditional crescent design fitted to the forward wheel splashers but the example seen here is one of a few provided with oval cabside plates bearing both the name and the engine's number. The engine is No. 3327 "Marco Polo" caught at Chester in April 1935 and withdrawn the following year. No. 3327 was one of the Bulldogs with curved frames; straight frames were introduced on the class commencing with No. 3341 in 1900.

Aberdare Class 2-6-0 No. 2676 running light near Oxford in 1935. These classic Dean engines were introduced in 1900 initially for work around the South Wales coalfields, hence their name. The type was given an extended life owing to World War Two and No. 2676 was not withdrawn until 1946; the last survivor following three years later

At Paddington, Oxford's No. 4979 "Wooton Hall" provides unusual motive power for the down Cathedrals Express normally worked by a Worcester Castle.

No. 6853 "Morehampton Grange" stands on an up express in the up loop platform at Birmingham's Snow Hill.

Castle Class 4-6-0 No. 7031 "Cromwell's Castle" stands on the down relief line at Reading General at the head of a down Worcester express.

Previous spread
Another golden moment from the football specials on 27th April 1963 when the semi final of the F.A. cup was played at Aston Villa's ground bringing 15 special trains from the Southampton area into Birmingham Snow Hill. Here, entering Snow Hill's up platform is Stanier 8F No. 48417 piloting No. 34039 "Boscastle" on the 07.43 a.m. from Southampton. In the down platform stands No. 34094, one of only two un-rebuilt Bullied Pacifics used on these specials.

Appropriately named Hawksworth 4-6-0 No. 1006 "County of Cornwall" stands in Penzance Station with an up express.

Castle Class 4-6-0 No.5089 "Westminster Abbey" pauses in Bristol Temple Meads with the up Cornishman 10.30 am Penzance to Wolverhampton. Note the bevy of train spotters immersed in their task.

At Birmingham Snow Hill, No.5955 "Garth Hall" of Didcot pauses with a down stopping train.

Previous spread
Crossing the River Dee at Chester, Class 5700 0-6-0PT No. 8730 heads an empty wagon train towards Saltney. These humble engines constituted Britain's largest class totalling 863 engines built between 1929 and 1949.

A Class 1400 0-4-2T propels a B.R. built railmotor trailer on the approach to Hightown with a Wrexham to Ellesmere service.

Another push and pull train, probably on a Stourbridge service, with a Class 6400, 0-6-0PT in charge. The railmotor trailers are of G.W.R. and B.R. design respectively whilst behind the engine is a former L.M.S. van and a covered goods wagon.